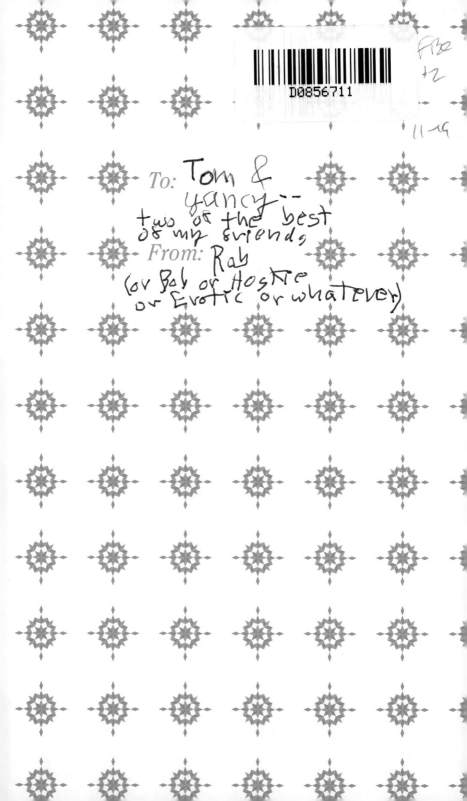

FB2
$2

11-19

To: Tom &
Yancy --
two of the best
of my friends,
From: Rab
(or Bob or Hoshie
or Erotic or whatever)

I cherish your
friendship.

Bob Hopkinson

3/26/96

IN TRIBUTE TO THE BRIDGES

Long-lived Lumber
(to all six remaining)

These old bridges have lasted decades—
Carriers across streams
Or shelters from the storm.
Palpable proof that people want immortality.
They built the bridges to last, didn't they?
With something of themselves hammered into each.
And those structures have indeed endured—
Even outlasted their builders;
Lasting longer than the lengthiest human lifespan.

Robert E. Hopkinson, Jr.

7/4/94

Mary MacKinnon Courtney

BRIDGES IN TIME - Keepsakes Celebrating the
Covered Bridges of Madison County

Editor: Becky Wayne Johnston
Designer: Robert Mickey Hager
Photographer: Craig Anderson
Typeset in Calfisch Script and Clearface

Printer: R. R. Donnelley & Sons Company
Printed in Mexico

ISBN: 0-9646870-0-3
10 9 8 7 6 5 4 3 2 1
First Edition

BRIDGES IN TIME

*Keepsakes Celebrating the Covered Bridges
of Madison County*

Landauer Books
Landauer Corporation
Cumming, Iowa

CONTENTS

G o west, young man, go west! The Homestead Act of 1862, precipitated a vast migration of pioneers. Lured by the promise of prosperity, these brave souls fanned out across the prairies.

After crossing the Ohio River and the mighty Mississippi, many homesteaded in Madison County, Iowa on land near rivers for a steady supply of water. Soon the countryside was dotted with primitive cabins.

With the building of most of the covered bridges in Madison County in the mid 1880's, pioneer families occasionally left the isolation of their log cabins to gather for quilting bees and regional fairs. At quilting bees women gathered over the comfort of the quilting frame to share tragedies and triumphs. They also exchanged quilt block piecing patterns, resulting in a myriad of colorful quilts that have been passed down from generations. Of the 19 covered bridges built in Madison County over a century ago to provide shelter from the storms, only six remain. And of thousands of quilts also constructed for warmth and comfort, only a few century quilts are to be found.

Talented artisans from Madison County commemorate these treasures from the past, preserving their memory for future generations. Well-known local artist Mary Courtney has rendered each of the remaining bridges in pen and ink. Resident poet Robert Hoskinson has contributed his poems composed about the bridges. The Madison County Historical Society, under the direction of Wendell Spencer, has graciously allowed the use of exquisite antique quilts from the Museum's collection. Several individual designers and collectors have also loaned prized quilts from the era of the building of the covered bridges. And nationally recognized quilters Marianne Fons and Liz Porter, with a group of fabric artisans organized into a modern-day quilting bee—the Madison County Quilt Company— contributed their folk-art Sampler.

To all of you we express our gratitude and heartfelt appreciation. This spirit of cooperation handed down from the early settlers allows us to bring you the heritage of Madison County—bridges in time!

—*Becky Johnston, Editor*

Madison County's Covered Bridges were utilitarian in origin, built for the comfort and convenience of the residents as they travelled through the countryside. With the building of the bridges, social connections for rural families formerly separated by distance and waterways were suddenly made possible. To preserve this new-found freedom in travel, unique coverings were constructed over the bridges, to protect the massive timbers from exposure to the elements—wind, rain, snow and sleet.

Inadvertently, the covered bridges provided shelter from the elements as well as from prying eyes for generations of Madison County lovers. Legends have been spun about the venerable old structures and what has gone on in them and around them for decades. Over time, the "Kissing Bridges" have become a symbol of romance in themselves and have lasted long enough to become as enduring and perennial as love itself.

Blend everything together and what you have is a recipe for wonder—wonder worthy of attention, as the bridges graphically connect the past with the present. The following poems were written out of reverence for the bridges—what they have meant in the past and what they mean for the future. I hope you enjoy the poetry and derive from it some measure of the historical and mystical aura which surrounds the bridges.

In the autumn of 1982 I wrote a poem dedicated to the Hogback and Holliwell Bridges. I'd like to share it with you as a poetical expression of what the Madison County Covered Bridges have meant to me and so many others down through the years.

Robert E. Hoskinson jr.

Hogback and Holliwell

Massive in their comfort,
The bridges stand aged and serene,
With thick beams weathered by drying winds
And innumerable lovers' vows carved deep,
With huge bolts pinning plank to brace—
Wooden floors worn smooth and splintered rough
By wheels and skids and hooves.
Countless travelers have paused
Within these great, wooden tunnels,
Sheltered from a storm overhead,
Safe above the rushing stream below...

Or simply imagining harsh weather
And the coziness of nestling secure
In a secluded corner
Out of the wind,
Warm and dry.

R. H.
10/2/82

Wooded With Waterways

This was the ocean's floor once,
And the evidence is everywhere —
Limestone is all around, maybe buried under the soil
sediment of decayed plants and animals,
But it's down there.
Sea animals lived here in an ocean
Millions of years ago;
As they died, their calcium shells drifted to rest
on the bottom on top of other shells.
That got heavy, heavy made heat,
And over the centuries shellstone formed
With shells in it.
Then the land pushed the water back
Leaving bare stone — limestone,
Plants grew upon it, animals did their part too,
they all followed the sea critters in death,
Covering the stone with a thick layer of soil,
camouflaging it so humans had to dig for it,
And people hereabouts did.
But the seasons didn't stop.

Waterstreams from rains and dews and melted snow
Sought a way through the soil,
First flowing straight,
Then winding more and more—in less of a hurry—with age.
There were lots of wooded hills here—
The glacier didn't make it this far,
The run-off was swift, making many streams,
And where there are many streams
Plus taming-minded humans,
There are many bridges.
So we have Madison County, Iowa:
Land of limestone and waterways and bridges.

R. H.
11/12/94

Madison County
quilt by Marty Freed

Assorted blocks
representing the
"best" of Madison
County include a
tribute to native-son
John Wayne, a
bridge, barns and
silos, cut-stone
country houses,
crops, livestock, and
the Red Delicious
apple originating and
grown in orchards
dotting the country-
side. A dozen blocks
each with a capital
letter are cleverly
arranged to form an
acrostic.

*Variation of a Pineapple Log Cabin antique quilt
courtesy of the Madison County Historical Society*

Symbolic of hospitality, the pineapple motif was
often used for the Log Cabin block in a technique
called "strip piecing." The combination is evident on
this antique century quilt which was pieced by Mrs.
Esther Pontius Beyer, and brought to Iowa by her
daughter Mrs. M. B. Travis, in 1879, from
Punxsutawney, Pennsylvania.

THE HOLLIWELL
COVERED BRIDGE

*"Truly a pooling place
for jubilation"*

Holliwell bridge — Madison County, Ia.

At 122 feet in length, the Holliwell Bridge is the longest of all the Covered Bridges with its construction unique among them—it is bow-backed. The bridge was built in 1880 by Benton Jones and C. K. Foster to span a river on a westward highway taken by many pioneers. The rough dwellings the pioneers built inspired quilt blocks composed of strips of fabric also arranged in interlocking rows. Traditional Log Cabin quilts have enjoyed enduring popularity in a multitude of variations. Often, patterns shared at quilting bees reflected the landscape of the times. A plowed field inspired Straight Furrows and beams of a new barn set in straight rows became Barn Raising.

Barn–like Bystander

Staring through cracks between floorboards
Toward the sun–splashed riverbed below,
It occurs to me
That this old bridge
Has witnessed an immense number of happinesses over the
years—
Truly a pooling place for jubilation.
From youngsters wading mired waist–deep in river mud
And shouting with glee
To the first kiss of young lovers
Followed by blissful relief,
Holliwell has seen so much
Worry dissolve into joy
It's become joyous itself.

Robert E. Hopkinson, jr.

8/21/94

Twilight Wreath quilt
by Marty Freed

A common characteristic of quilts from the mid 1800's was the choice of white for the background color. Wreaths with delicate florals were a favorite theme for the appliqué. The crowning glory of this reproduction quilt from that era is the spectacular butterfly quilted in the center of the elaborate wreath. One of 24 quilts in the appliqué division, Twilight Wreath was awarded Best of Show at the Iowa State Fair in 1993.

Sherry Said So*

Sherry speaks
Of this old, bow-backed bridge
With such reverence —
Of Holliwell's glory
And the sounds of butterflies out here.
Perhaps you can hear butterflies singing
Near the river bank
Or perhaps not,
It doesn't matter.
For without question this is an enchanted place,
And Sherry can hear the filmy fluttering
Of dozens of wispy wings —
It gives her peace.
While the bridge beckons,
Luring you into a long hallway
Leading to the other side of the river.

*and that's good enough for me

Robert E. Hopkinson, jr.
11/4/93

Variation of a Double Irish Chain antique quilt courtesy of Marty Freed

This handsome variation of a Double Irish Chain antique century quilt was purchased with a scrap of tattered paper pinned to it. The note written in faded pencil read, "Dell Haines made this quilt when she was 16—she was born in 1868."

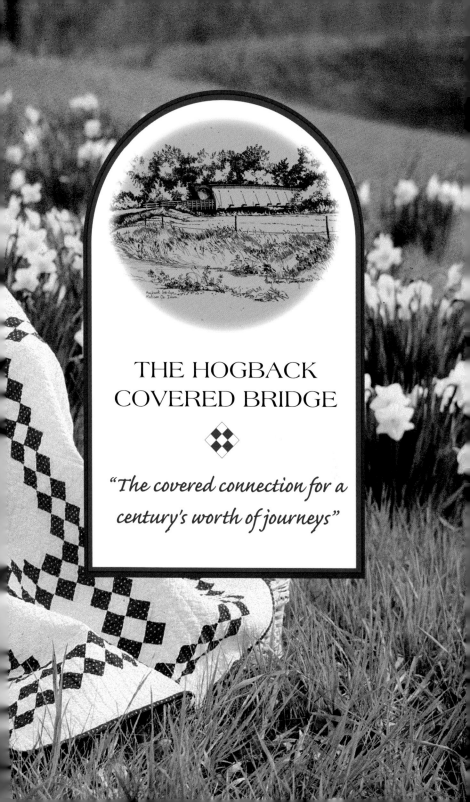

THE HOGBACK
COVERED BRIDGE

❖

*"The covered connection for a
century's worth of journeys"*

Hogback bridge,
Madison Co. Iowa

For more than a century, the Hogback Covered Bridge has remained in its original location and in regular use until its recent refurbishment. Although most bridges were named for the families who lived nearby, this bridge takes its name from a style of construction—the slightly arched covering is of hogbacked or cambered roof construction. Likewise, many of the patchwork utility quilts that have withstood over a hundred years of wear and tear are identified by their particular style of construction. The early quilts like the Irish Chain were simple geometric shapes cut from scraps of clothing and linens.

Timeworn Windbreaker

After walking into a cold wind
For what seems like forever,
Being inside Hogback's windbreak walls
Feels wonderful.
I guess this is what they mean
By wind chill.
Your face,
Unbearably shrunken moments ago
Instantly regains it shape.
This floor-saver bridge wasn't put up as a shelter
But that's how it turned out—
In all kinds of weather.
A beacon for foot-weary wanderers
For decades:
Always there if you wanted
To cross the river—
On horseback or in a motorcar—
Or just sit a while with someone special.
And there are pigeons cooing under the south eve.

Robert E. Hopkinson, jr.
11/19/94

Hogback Heavenly

Basking on the riverbank
In sweet, spring sunshine
Surrounded by soul–soothing sounds
From the river as it spilled
Over rocky shallows into deeper water,
I could see half a mile downstream
With nothing in the way.
Shifting shadows on the fine, sand soil
Beneath a refurbished Hogback Bridge
Hovered like a memory–mist
Rich with recollection,
Slipping along the bank
In slow motion,
As the sun rose in its upward arc,
And breezes stirred budding branches
On young trees.
Nearby was a concrete, by–pass bridge,
Wide and smooth and gray,
Sitting upon massive supports—
Beautiful in its own way
But paling by comparison
With its old counterpart:

The covered connection
For a century's worth of journeys—
And, unintentionally,
The covered confidante
For a full measure of private passion.

Robert E. Hopkinson, jr.
4/18/94

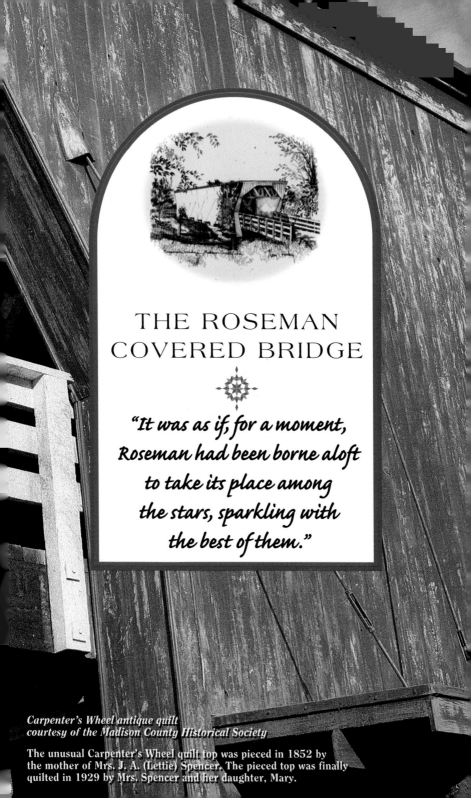

THE ROSEMAN COVERED BRIDGE

*"It was as if, for a moment,
Roseman had been borne aloft
to take its place among
the stars, sparkling with
the best of them."*

*Carpenter's Wheel antique quilt
courtesy of the Madison County Historical Society*

The unusual Carpenter's Wheel quilt top was pieced in 1852 by
the mother of Mrs. J. A. (Lettie) Spencer. The pieced top was finally
quilted in 1929 by Mrs. Spencer and her daughter, Mary.

The Roseman Bridge, built in 1883 by Benton Jones, is the subject of local legend and supposedly haunted. The Roseman is also unique as the only remaining covered bridge still in its natural setting. With no modern by-pass bridge nearby, the rugged bridge and the area surrounding it stands as a strong, silent tribute to simpler times. Likewise, the Carpenter's Wheel quilt shown with the Roseman Bridge, brings back memories of skilled tradesmen of yesteryear. Their expert use of basic tools resulted in the construction of massive structures that still stand in testimony to their labors of love.

After the Storm Has Passed

Despite the rushing river's fury
Swollen by many a storm
Over the years,
Roseman has remained—
Sage and silent and safe.
While the bridge was being built,
The stream ran bankful after a rain,
Washing the lumber away,
But never again
When it was done.
It's withstood the onslaught
Of weather changes
For a century
Without a whimper—
And even now it must be wondering
What all the recent hub-bub has been about,
Seems to be leaning just slightly
Into the north wind
As if bracing
For fresh gusts of human curiosity
That're bound to blow,
People coming to ponder
The reasons for Roseman's enduring charm,
The secret of its long-lasting life.
Why hasn't it caved in?
Under the umbrella of a starspell?
Or maybe there's some sort of magic potion
in the riverwater?

R. H.
11/8/94

Roseman on a Clear Night

The still night air was filled with fireflies,
And their constant twinkling
Lit an outline of the bridge's boundaries.
It was moonless, but thousands of stars shone brightly...
Away from the gaudy glow of yardlights,
The darkness was pure, with no clouds and no wind.
The "Haunted Bridge":
Legend has it that once a sheriff's posse
Chased a thief out here.
With part of the posse hot on his heels
And another part dead ahead,
The robber entered the bridge,
Maybe on a night like this,
And vanished without a trace.
More recently, the old bridge
Was distinguished as a magical place
In a well–told tale of star-crossed lovers.
Pretty glorious billings for a passageway
Whose time has passed
And sits at a dead end
On an obscure country road.

But on this night,
As I watched intently,
Earthbound fireflies seemed to lift the bridge up.
It was as if,
For a moment,
Roseman had been borne aloft
To take its place among the stars,
Sparkling with the best of them.

Robert E. Hopkinson jr.
8/7/93

Roseman Bridge quilt
by Kris Kerrigan

This contemporary rendition of the Roseman Bridge is a charming blend of the old and the new. The small-scale quilt is sized for wall hanging. Design motifs are appliquéd and then accented with trims for a three-dimensional effect. The border is an old-fashioned quilt pattern—Contrary Wife.

*Scrap Inventory
Reduction Star quilt
by Marty Freed*

**Modeled after the
pioneer tradition of
saving scraps until
enough had been
collected to create
an entire quilt, this
modern interpretation
features Star blocks
bordered with strip
piecing.**

Starship Roseman

Like a stone hurled with strength
Into the distance,
The old bridge seems caught
In galactic flow
Toward a faraway destiny,
Bursting the bonds
That have held it anchored
Over the streambed for years,
Sailing away on the wings
Of legend and hard use.

Robert E. Hotkinson jr.
8/9/93

Variation of a Windmill antique pieced top quilted by Marty Freed

Pieced tops, like this Windmill variation, often spent years in a trunk or chest of drawers until someone took time to bind the top to a backing with quilting. Marty purchased this antique top for $12 at the Mabel Chew sale in Madison County and then lovingly completed it with hours of hand-quilting.

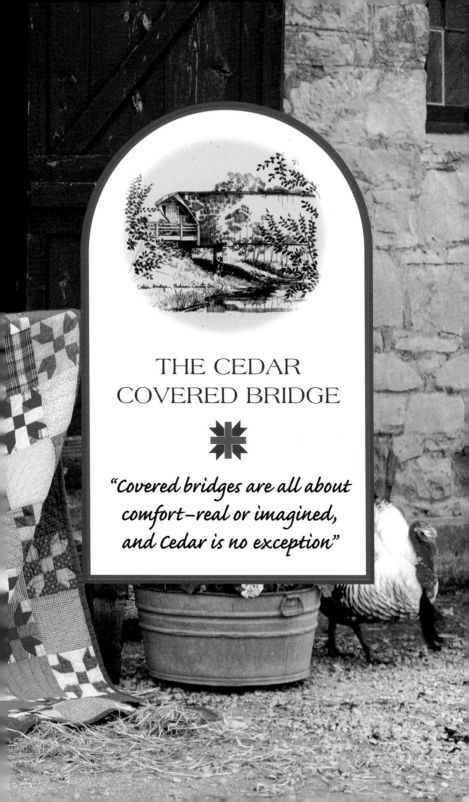

THE CEDAR COVERED BRIDGE

"Covered bridges are all about comfort—real or imagined, and Cedar is no exception"

Cedar Bridge, Madison County Ia

Mary Courtney

Originally known as the Casper Bridge, this covered bridge eventually took on the name of the Cedar Creek over which it was built in1883 by Benton Jones. Later the Cedar Covered Bridge was moved to a park east of there where it now spans the same creek as it leaves Cedar Lake. It is the only remaining covered bridge that can be driven through—all the others are open only to foot traffic. Many Madison County treasures share the same history. The Cedar Bridge, like the Windmill pieced top from the Mabel Chew sale, has been moved around, restored, or even rebuilt, but still remains intact in the heart of Madison County.

✳ CEDAR BRIDGE ✳

Safe In the Center

The old bridge was lifted
Out of familiar surroundings—
Taken out of time, really,
When it was moved,
And everything around it now
Feels make-believe,
Almost ethereal.
What better place to pretend?
Imagine an immense snowstorm.
Both ends of Cedar are drifted shut,
The wind's gusting,
And snow is thick in the air.
You can feel the storm—see it, hear it,
But it can't reach you
Where you are in the middle of the bridge.
The rugged roof and cross-work walls
Protect you.
You can venture to the edge of the drifts—
Even stand in them,
But you can always retreat to bridge center
Where the air is calm
And the floor is dry.
Covered bridges are all about comfort—
Real or imagined,
And Cedar is no exception.

Robert E. Hopkinson, Jr.

11/13/94

*Postage Stamp
antique quilt
courtesy of
Melva Bucksbaum*

Girls as young as ten often began practicing their piecing with scraps of worn fabrics cut into small squares. Composed of 3,465 one-half-inch squares of scrap fabric, this quilt was started in 1895 and completed the following year by Eva Warren Wentzell—her first quilt project at the age of 13.

Utilitarian Wildflower

It spanned Cedar Creek
First at one end of the lake and then the other.
Before, it was gateway to Winterset
From the north,
Now, it's center stage in a park
Near the Country Club.
Traffic got too heavy where it was built,
So, in fear the bridge might give out,
It was moved—
To preserve history, I suppose,
But probably not with an eye for its beauty.
Half a dozen kinds of wildflowers
Are blooming around it today,
But Cedar Bridge blooms brightest:
A stunning relic of times past,
Standing in the humid heat amid
The lingering smell of old creosote
And the sound of rushing water
In the creek below—
The whole scene presided over
By the sheltering branches of walnut and burr oak.

Robert E. Hodgson, Jr.

8/14/93

Iowa Star in Four Seasons quilt
by Marty Freed

The seasons are so distinct in Iowa, that it only seemed appropriate for a master quilter like Marty Freed to piece the Iowa Star block in four separate strips. They range from light to dark, with each strip representing a season—winter, spring, summer and autumn.

THE IMES
COVERED BRIDGE

"Suddenly there was Imes Bridge, strong and silent and safe—and mystical."

Oldest of the six remaining structures, the Imes Covered Bridge has survived over a century's worth of Iowa's constantly changing seasons like those worked in fabric on the Iowa Star in Four Seasons quilt. The Imes Bridge was built in 1870 and moved 17 years later to the Imes Crossing on Clanton Creek. After many years of service, Imes was retired to a roadside park in the nearby town of St. Charles.

✦ IMES BRIDGE ✦

Roadway Renewal

When travelers on county backroads
Thought they were lost for sure,
Convinced the road led nowhere,
Suddenly there was Imes Bridge,
Strong and silent and safe—and mystical.
The sloping roof above bolted beams
Kept its floor dry and the way clear,
And "Something this refined can't be far from someplace."
It's in a roadside park now, and
From inside the bridge at this moment,
I can see fluffy clouds drifting in a blue sky
Through the space
Between its latticed boards and shingled eaves,
And it's as though I'm floating away with the bridge
To become part of an eternal cloudcover,
Imes stretching and changing as much as any cloud formation
Buffeted by the breeze.

9/11/93

39

THE CUTLER-DONAHOE COVERED BRIDGE

✾

"This is more than merely a passageway—it's a royal room with a high ceiling."

*Variation of a Rose of Sharon appliqué antique quilt
courtesy of Jackie Leckband*

Since appliqué was so time consuming, it was reserved for ladies of leisure and became a symbol of affluence and status in the community. Green or turkey red on white is the predominate color for an antebellum legacy such as this exquisite heirloom century quilt—certainly a lasting tribute to a bygone era.

Cutler-Donahoe bridge
Madison County, Ia.

Mary Courtney 93

Like the well-preserved Rose of Sharon century quilt that may date back to the
Civil War era, the Cutler-Donahoe Covered Bridge was built to last with a
unique set of wooden pins holding it together. Cutler-Donahoe bears the names
of two families closely involved with the bridge Eli Cox constructed in 1871 at
its original location northeast of Winterset in Madison County. Nearly a century
after it was completed the wooden pins still held, and the Cutler-Donahoe
Covered Bridge was moved eighteen miles to a city park in Winterset.

Within the Confines of Cutler-Donahoe

Pitched roof designed to pour
Rainwater back into the river
And protect the bridgeboard flooring from the weather,
Air flows constantly through here —
probably always has.
It's almost as if the bridge is alive,
Drawing the breeze in one end of its lumber-length,
Shaping it into something square-lovely.
And sighing it out the other.
The wind curls under wood-shingled eaves,
Fills the open space between wall and roof,
Bounces off delicate-rugged braces
That look like lattice-lace from a distance.
This is more than merely a passageway—
It's a royal room with a high ceiling
Where breeze sounds are part of things
And reverberate top to bottom
As though oozing from the wooden walls
Of this timeless echo chamber.

Robert E. Hokinson, sr.

8/14/93

Flowering Heart appliqué wall hanging
by Jackie Leckband

When pioneer women needed a circle for a design element
they often used a penny as a template. To make a rug,
penny-sized circles were cut from wool scraps and stitched
onto a long-wearing wool backing piece. These "penny
rugs" as they became known were the inspiration for wool-
on-wool appliqué. The use of circles was expanded to
include birds, hearts, and floral borders as in this modern
interpretation of an old-fashioned art form.

Reflections Upon McBride

A stalwart refuge for buggy and wagon,
McBride Bridge connected
Both sides of the river for years.
But its usefulness waned,
And when a new roadbed was crowned,
The antique tunnel was carefully by-passed.
Then it burned.
Now only its remains stand proud,
Charred by bundles of bridgeboards
Hanging askew on empty pilings,
Attesting to the bridge's toughness,
And in spite of everything,
Its memory lives on.
If observers squint an eye just right,
McBride's sturdy frame still stands:
A shadowy silhouette against the sky,
Indelible testimony to times past.

Robert E. Hopkinson, Jr.
9/5/85

To Those That Were

Only six remain in this county—
Vestiges of former times,
But there were many other covered bridges here.
And those that are gone
Held the same charm and comfort
For weary travelers—
Or lovers looking for a private place—
As those that survived
To become the designated darlings
Of more modern days.
Some burned—leaving empty pilings,
Some simply rotted away—
Leaving little evidence of ever having been,
But they all spanned streams,
And they all were put together
By folks who also built barns.
Great barns built over wide riverbeds,
So stood the covered bridges that were—
Carefully constructed of beams
Balancing above bridgeboards,

IN MEMORY OF THE BRIDGES

Leaning into one another and the wind
To create places of rugged, roofed sturdiness
Even the elements couldn't bring down.
And the soulful silence that surrounds their memory
Permeates everything
As we honor those that still are.

R. H.
11/30/93

Madison County Sampler quilt
by the Madison County Quilt Company

Each block on this contemporary wall quilt is a pictorial tribute to Iowa and Madison County. The Iowa state flower—the wild rose—and even rattlesnakes, go hand-in-hand with the apples, barns and bridges that abound in Madison County.

47

Baltimore Album Memory quilt
by Jo Ann Allen

Reminiscent of album quilts originating in Baltimore around 1840, this quilt won Best of Show at the 1994 Iowa State Fair and at the Madison County Covered Bridge Festival in October of that same year. In album quilts each block is dedicated to preserving memories of family and friendships. Jo Ann chose the ship block in memory of her great-grandparents who emigrated from Wales. The corner blocks each represent the four greatest loves of Jo Ann's life—her husband, and three sons.

SENTIMENTS TO SHARE
OF MEMORIES IN TIME

Preserved for future generations with a unique wooden covering, the bridges of Madison County were a treasure hidden for more than a century in the heartland of America. Suddenly, through the pages of a simple story of enduring love, the Covered Bridges have captured the hearts of romantics around the world.

Just as the Covered Bridges of Madison County have gained unprecedented attention through a chance encounter, many of our most memorable encounters may be brief and even seemingly insignificant in the routine of daily life. However, when woven into the fabric of our lives, these often unanticipated moments in time become the blocks of memories that are arranged into a pattern that is uniquely ours. When pieced and quilted together, they are an enduring reflection of the past and the present blended almost imperceptibly into a celebration of life lived to the fullest.

Like a living stream, the current of our lives gathers momentum as we experience peaks and valleys along the journey. While we are carried by the stream, we seldom are able to look back or ahead, we can only live in the present. But if we momentarily step out of the stream, and stand on the bridge above, we can look back, recollecting with fondness memorable encounters of the past. Thus, these moments in time become bridges of memories that strengthen us. Standing firm upon these bridges, we can rise above our circumstances, gathering courage and renewed perspective. Reassured by the anchors of our past, we can resume living passionately in the present.

As you reflect back on chance encounters with people or places who have touched your life in a special way, we encourage you to use the following pages to express in your own words those sentiments of memories in time. They can be yours to hold in your heart for now. Later, they can be shared with future generations who also seek to blend an understanding of the past with the present to gain strength and renewed hope for tomorrow.

God wove a web of loveliness,
Of clouds and stars and birds,
But made not anything at all
So beautiful as words.
                    Ann Hempstead Branch

My memories of: _____

_____

_____

_____

_____

_____

_____

_____

_____

_____

_____

_____

_____

_____

_____

_____

_____

_____

_____

_____

_____

_____

_____

_____

_____

For what they'd never told me of,
And what I never knew;
It was that all the time, my love,
Love would be merely you.
Robert Brooke

My memories of: _____

_____
_____
_____
_____
_____
_____
_____
_____
_____
_____
_____
_____
_____
_____
_____
_____
_____
_____
_____
_____
_____
_____
_____

There is a destiny that makes us brothers:
None goes his way alone:
All that we send into the lives of others
Comes back into our own.
                    Edwin Markham

My memories of: _____

_____
_____
_____
_____
_____
_____
_____
_____
_____
_____
_____
_____
_____
_____
_____
_____
_____
_____
_____
_____
_____
_____

All that we need to do,
Be we low or high,
Is to see that we grow
Nearer the sky.
Lizette Woodworth Reese

My memories of: _____

_____

_____

_____

_____

_____

_____

_____

_____

_____

_____

_____

_____

_____

_____

_____

_____

_____

_____

_____

Nestled in the heartland of America, Iowa's most well-known county traces its origins to 1846 when it was named after the fourth President of the United States. Three years later, Madison County boasted of a burgeoning first census count of 701 residents!

The county commissioners met that same year to select a county seat. According to a fascinating history compiled by Lloyd H. Smith for the Madison County Historical Society, arguments waxed back and forth as to what to call the new town:

"Some said 'Summerset' or perhaps 'Somerset.' However, it being a rather cold day, one of the men slightly under the influence of John Barleycorn spoke up and said, 'Summerset, indeed, this place had better be called Winterset.' And so it is called 'Winterset' to this day because the name found a responsive chord in the hearts of the people."

When the county seat town of Winterset was laid out, the streets were all neatly arranged around a courthouse square in the center of town. The first courthouse was an 18x30-foot log cabin built at a cost of $150.00. That first temple of justice was also used for school, church, and later move away and used for a stable.

COURT HOUSE.

Building of the second courthouse, shown at right, commenced in 1868. It was built of the famed gray limestone so abundant in the county, in the form of a Greek Cross. Unfortunately, that courthouse burned in 1875. Its replacement is shown below. Also built from gray stone, the Madison County courthouse which remains in use today, was built on the foundation of its predecessor as strictly fireproof as possible from stone, brick, concrete, and metal for the dome. On the apex of the dome is a cupola, in which is "the town clock," having on its four sides face dials that are lighted at night and plainly visible for many miles. Historian Smith notes that, "At its completion, the courthouse was considered the best building of its kind in all the territory west of Chicago. A resident of the community when the building was completed wrote: 'Upon close inspection of the work of these fine craftsmen, one

cannot but be impressed with the perfection of their work and the skill required in the execution. True level and perpendicular lines are everywhere apparent. The sweeping curves of the beautiful arches are no where distorted by unequal settlement of inadequate foundations, in fact, the thick masonry walls and deep laid footings of the basement and the solid brick arches supporting the floors above, suggest the interior of a fortress.'"

Like the courthouse whose origins date back to a log cabin, many of the residents lived in log homes prior to building permanent residences from limestone. Many of these outstanding stone houses were built during the previctorian era, starting in the middle 1850's just before the Civil War. Caleb Clark and his wife came to Winterset and in 1854 started their stone house on South Eighth Avenue. In this first stone house in Winterset lived a little girl, Mary Clark, who was the first white child to be born in Madison County.

While many of the residents lived in log cabins or the stone houses, one distinguished citizen, Dr. C. D. Bevington, in 1856 built the elaborate mansion shown at left, on a hilltop overlooking Winterset. More than a century later, this grand home was a gift of June Kaser to the Madison County Historical Society. It has been restored to its Victorian richness by a dedicated group of volunteers and is now on the National Historic Register as is the nearby walnut-paneled stone privy and stone barn with black walnut interior framing that were also built by Dr. Bevington. Quoining was a commonly used method in the building of early stone structures. Alternating ends and sides of rectangular stones at each of

the corners gives a classic appearance as well as strength to the structure as evidenced by the old North River stone schoolhouse, below, built in 1874 and now restored. Another interesting stone structure in Madison County is the Clark Tower—a stone tower that Ross Rogers, grandson of Caleb Clark, helped build as a memorial to his grandparents. Of course the limestone quarries also provided ample stone for the headstones of the many graves in some fifty cemeteries scattered over the county. Without modern medicine and hygiene, the average life expectancy for early pioneers was a mere 30 years of age. As the historian points out, with such slow travel over almost impassable roads, in all kinds of weather, it was imperative that the cemeteries be close at hand. So through those struggling years the family grave yards were founded close by all over the county. However, the cemetery of the St. Patrick Parish in Lee township has a different reason for its location. The early settlers there were having a discussion as to whether or not the church, shown at left, and the cemetery should be located on the north or the south side of North River. The argument went on and on. Finally an old man, a government surveyor, returning from further west became ill. He stopped to rest at the home of Patrick Walsh and died on the south side of the river. While Mr. Walsh and some of his neighbors left to locate a burial place, a half dozen men from the north side of the river slipped in and took the corpse and started the cemetery on the north side of the river.

Soon afterwards in the summer of 1856—over a century ago—the church was built near the grave. The church and the graveyard thus started have been serving the good people of the 'Irish Settlement' for many years.

John Cutler, a boy of 15 years of age, who was left to guard the body of the old surveyor lived to be 99 years old. He died in 1930 and lies buried in St. Patricks and the Cutler-Donahoe Covered Bridge at left, is named in his honor.

While many residents experienced relative comfort in Winterset and other surrounding towns, other brave souls home-steaded in rural areas of Madison County on land near rivers for a steady supply of water. Soon the countryside was dotted with primitive cabins and pioneers who needed access to nearby towns for supplies. With the building of most of the covered bridges in Madison County in the mid 1880's, rivers became crossable, allowing pioneer families to occasionally leave the isolation of their log cabins to travel by horse and wagon to town or to gather for quilting bees and regional fairs.

Many of the original bridges became obsolete because they were built only for foot or horse traffic and were not strong enough or wide enough for the weight and size of modern trans-portation and machin-ery. When a new by-pass bridge was built, like the construction down-stream from the Rose-Dunmire Covered Bridge, often the old bridge was torn down. But, six survive and one bridge, the Cedar Covered Bridge, can still be driven through with modern vehicles.

The Red Delicious apple has its origins in Madison County. Historian Lloyd C. Smith attributes it to a Quaker farmer, Jesse Hiatt, who came to Madison County in 1856. "In the early 1880's he planted an apple orchard. It was composed of Bellflower seedlings. One seedling came up out of line with the other trees and Mr. Hiatt cut it down. He liked straight symmetrical rows. However, the seedling came up a second time and again Mr. Hiatt cut it down. A third time the little sprout came up and this time Mr. Hiatt said, 'Thee shall grow.'"

"It did grow and the first crop was one apple. Mr. Hiatt sent some of the apples to a fruit fair, and one of the judges who bit into this new apple said, 'Um Yum, Delicious,' and that is how the Delicious apple got its name." The original tree, shown above, "lived and produced fruit until 1940 when it succumbed to the Armistice Day storm as did many other apple trees in the state of Iowa."

Famous places often go hand-in-hand with famous faces. In addition  to the Red Delicious apple and Covered Bridges, another Madison County attraction is the birthplace of John Wayne. The Duke was born Marion Robert Morrison on May 26, 1907, in a modest home in Winterset now open for tours.

Madison County's Historical Sites

Amazingly enough, the pioneer spirit, conservation and preservation have resulted in 45 pieces of property that are recorded on the National Register of Historic Places.

• Cumming	St. Patrick's Church
	(The Pope visited this Irish settlement on October 4, 1979.)
• Earlham	James Allen Stone Barn
	Earlham Public School
	John Early and Elizabeth McMurn House
	W. T. Ford House
	Daniel Henderson and Nancy Swaford House
	Peter McQuie and Isabelle McCulloch Milk House
	Seth and Elizabeth Wilson House
• Macksburg	J. D. Craven, Women's Relief Corps Halls
• Peru	William Ogburn House
• St. Charles	John S. Homes and Elizabeth Beem Barn
	Imes Covered Bridge
	Hogan Queen and Martha Runkle House
• Winterset	George Armstrong and Susan Guiberson House
	C. D. Bevington and Eliza Heath Privy
	C. D. Bevington House and Stone Barn
	Cedar Covered Bridge
	Seymour Church House
	W. J. and Nettie J. Cornell House
	Cutler-Donahoe Covered Bridge

The Cedar Bridge

The Cutler-Donahoe Bridge

The Hogback Bridge

Madison County's Historical Sites

Winterset (continued...) John Drake and Amanda Bigler House
Duff Barn
John M. Duncan House
Henry Evans and Elizabeth Adkinson House
Edwin R. Guiberson House
Hogback Covered Bridge
Holliwell Covered Bridge
Emily Hornback House
Legacy in Stone: The Settlement Era of
Madison County, Iowa Thematic Resources
John Andrew and Sara Macumber Ice House
McDonald House
Madison County Courthouse City Square
William Anzi Nichols House
North River Stone Schoolhouse
Roseman Covered Bridge
John Schnellbacher and Fredericka
Meyer House
Nicholas Schoenenberger House and Barn
William R. Shriver and Martha Foster House
Hiram C. Smith House
Hiram C. Smith Milking Shed
Sprague, Brown and Knowlton Store
Miller Richard Tidrick and Mary Fisher House
J. G. and Elizabeth S. Vawter House
Munger White and Co. Store

The Holliwell Bridge

The Imes Bridge

The Roseman Bridge

ACKNOWLEDGMENTS

We are grateful to the many people who have worked to make this book possible. We extend our special thanks to The Madison County Historical Society, under the direction of Wendell Spencer, for graciously allowing the use of several exquisite antique quilts from the Museum's collection. Several individual designers and collectors have also loaned prized quilts and we offer our heartfelt thanks to the following:

Quilt Sources:

Jo Ann Allen—cover; 48; 50-53

Melva Bucksbaum—34

Marty Freed—cover; 9; 14; 16-17; 28; 30-31; 36-37

Kris Kerrigan—27

Jackie Leckband—40-41; 44

Madison County Quilt Company (Marianne Fons, Marty Freed, Kris Kerrigan, Jackie Leckband, Eden Pearson, Liz Porter)—47

The Madison County Historical Society, Winterset, IA— cover; 10-11; 22-23

Photo Locations:

Madison County Historical Complex, Winterset, IA—9; 14; 27; 30-31

The Covered Bridges of Madison County—cover; 3; 10-11; 20-23; 40-41

Landauer Corporation—16-17; 36-37

Flowers:

Floral design by Cody Evett of Boesen The Florist, Des Moines, IA

Photographs:

Craig Anderson—cover; 3; 9; 10-11; 14; 16-17; 21; 22-23; 27; 28; 30-31; 34; 36-37; 40-41; 44; 47; 48

Gene Crawford, Larry's Photography—55-61

Mark Davitt—57 (St. Patrick's Church)

All others courtesy of The Madison County Historical Society

SOURCE LIST

Patterns for selected quilts and wall hangings are available from
the following sources:

Jo Ann Allen
Rural Route 1
St. Charles, IA 50240
515/462-2056

Marty Freed
Rural Route 1, Box 179
Winterset, IA 50273
515/462-1704

Kris Kerrigan
BUTTON WEEDS
1275 Pheasant Avenue
Afton, IA 50830
515/347-8831

Jackie Leckband
THE FOLK ART SHOP
333 Fifth Street
West Des Moines, IA 50265
515/274-1419

Madison County Quilt Company
1275 Pheasant Avenue
Afton, IA 50830
515/347-8831